Soul songs

Exploring love, temptation, guilt and fear from the Psalms

by Tim Chester

Soul songs
A Good Book Guide on the Psalms
© Tim Chester/The Good Book Company, 2006. Reprinted 2011, 2014, 2015, 2016.

The Good Book Company
Tel (UK): 0333 123 0880
Tel: (US): 866 244 2165
Email: info@thegoodbook.co.uk

Websites
UK: www.thegoodbook.co.uk
N America: www.thegoodbook.com
Australia: www.thegoodbook.com.au
New Zealand: www.thegoodbook.co.nz

Unless indicated, all Scripture references are taken from the HOLY BIBLE, NEW INTERNATIONAL VERSION. Copyright © 1973, 1978, 1984, 2011 by Biblica, Inc. Used by permission. All rights reserved worldwide.

ISBN: 9781904889960

All rights reserved. Except as may be permitted by the Copyright Act, no part of this publication may be reproduced in any form or by any means without prior permission from the publisher.

Printed in the Czech Republic

CONTENTS

Introduction: Good Book Guides

Every Bible-study group is different—yours may take place in a church building, in a home or in a cafe, on a train, over a leisurely mid-morning coffee or squashed into a 30-minute lunch break. Your group may include new Christians, mature Christians, non-Christians, mums and tots, students, businessmen or teens. That's why we've designed these *Good Book Guides* to be flexible for use in many different situations.

Our aim in each session is to uncover the meaning of a passage, and see how it fits into the "big picture" of the Bible. But that can never be the end. We also need to appropriately apply what we have discovered to our lives. Let's take a look at what is included:

Talkabout: Most groups need to "break the ice" at the beginning of a session, and here's the question that will do that. It's designed to get people talking around a subject that will be covered in the course of the Bible study.

Investigate: The Bible text for each session is broken up into manageable chunks, with questions that aim to help you understand what the passage is about. **The Leader's Guide** contains **guidance on questions**, and sometimes additional "follow-up" questions.

Explore more (optional): These questions will help you connect what you have learned to other parts of the Bible, so you can begin to fit it all together like a jig-saw; or occasionally look at a part of the passage that's not dealt with in detail in the main study.

Apply: As you go through a Bible study, you'll keep coming across **apply** sections. These are questions to get the group discussing what the Bible teaching means in practice for you and your church. **Getting personal** is an opportunity for you to think, plan and pray about the changes that you personally may need to make as a result of what you have learned.

Pray: We want to encourage prayer that is rooted in God's word—in line with his concerns, purposes and promises. So each session ends with an opportunity to review the truths and challenges highlighted by the Bible study, and turn them into prayers of request and thanksgiving.

The **Leader's Guide** and introduction provide historical background information, explanations of the Bible texts for each session, ideas for **optional extra** activities, and guidance on how best to help people uncover the truths of God's word.

Why study *Soul songs*?

Have you ever got the tune of a mindless song stuck in your head? You find yourself humming a song you don't even like. The world around us sings a song and that song often gets fixed in our minds. We find ourselves joining in. What the world thinks and desires becomes what we think and desire.

The Psalms help us re-tune our hearts. David says that the Lord "put a new song in my mouth, a hymn of praise to our God. Many will see and fear the LORD and put their trust in him" (Psalm 40 v 3). The Psalms re-tune our hearts to the new song of God's redemption. As a result, we learn again to fear God instead of fearing other people. We learn to trust God in the face of adversity.

> *The law of the LORD is perfect, refreshing the soul.*
> *The statutes of the LORD are trustworthy,*
> *making wise the simple.*
> *The precepts of the LORD are right, giving joy to the heart.*
> *The commands of the LORD are radiant, giving light to*
> *the eyes. (Psalm 19 v 7-8)*

The word of God revives the soul like medicine. That is the theme of this selection of psalms. They are all taken from the first book of Psalms (Psalms 1 – 41), most of which are songs of people in trouble. They usually begin with the problems we face. But they don't leave us there. They turn us back to God; to his character and his salvation. They offer us hope in the midst of despair. They put a new song in our mouths.

You may feel as if your soul is afflicted, downcast or sick. You may be troubled by worry, sin, problems, suffering, fear or guilt. But in these psalms we will find medicine for the soul. We will learn with the psalmist to re-tune our hearts with the new song of God's redemption. And we will discover that the chorus of this new song is "Worthy is the Lamb" (Revelation 5 v 9-13).

These Bible studies offer more of a thematic journey through selected psalms, rather than an attempt to gain a complete understanding of each of these Spirit-inspired songs. The studies focus on aspects of the psalms that relate to our emotional response to the God who loved us and gave himself for us in Christ.

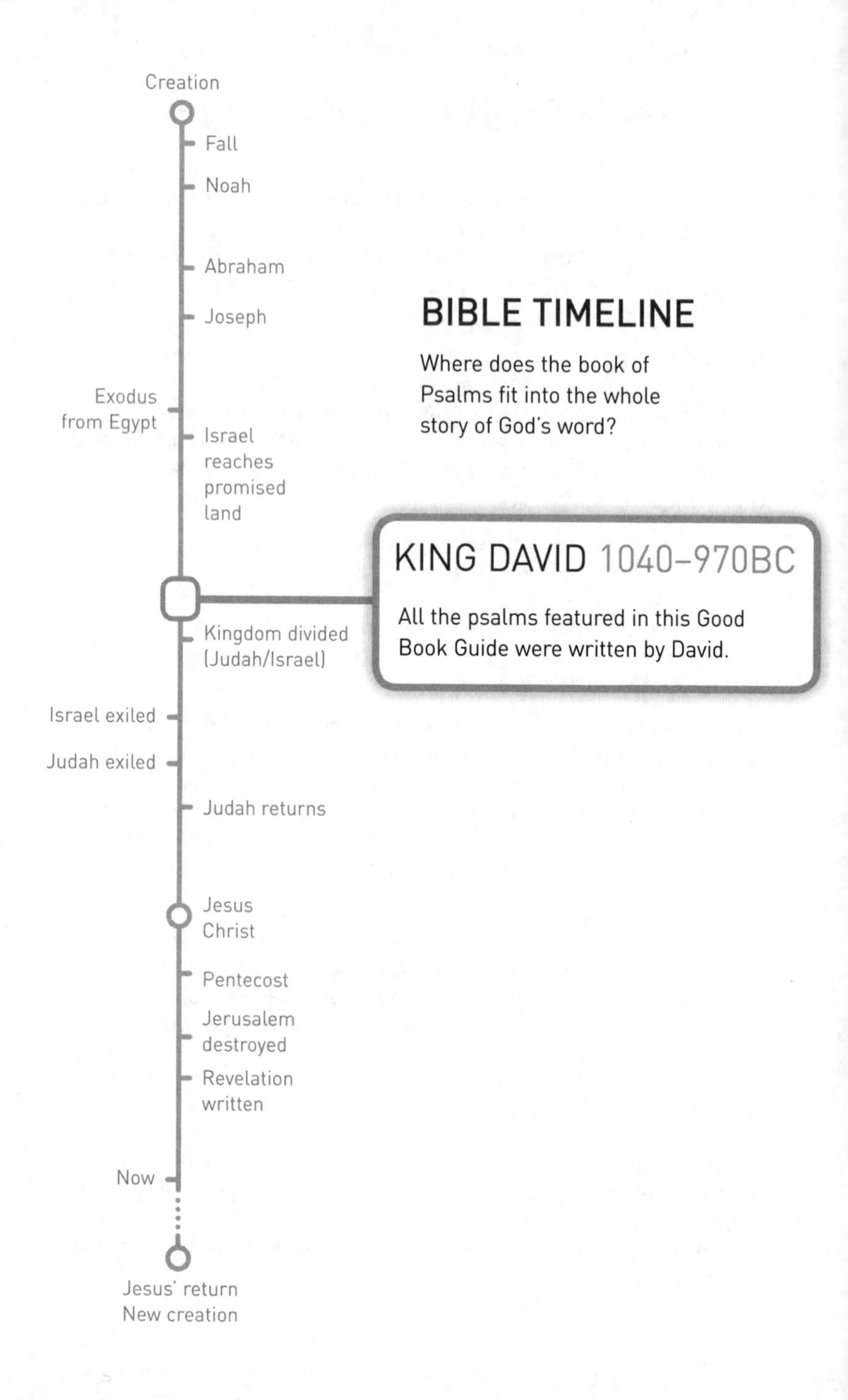
Creation
Fall
Noah
Abraham
Joseph
Exodus from Egypt
Israel reaches promised land
Kingdom divided (Judah/Israel)
Israel exiled
Judah exiled
Judah returns
Jesus Christ
Pentecost
Jerusalem destroyed
Revelation written
Now
Jesus' return New creation
BIBLE TIMELINE
Where does the book of Psalms fit into the whole story of God's word?
KING DAVID 1040–970BC
All the psalms featured in this Good Book Guide were written by David.

1

Psalms 3 and 4

A SONG FOR SLEEPLESS NIGHTS

talkabout

1. What thoughts or feelings keep you awake at night?

investigate

Read 2 Samuel 15 v 1-30

2. What is David's situation?

DICTIONARY

Absalom (v 1): one of King David's sons.
Zadok (v 24): the high priest.
Ark of the covenant of God (v 24): a gold-covered box where God was particularly present among his people.

3. What do you think you would have been thinking if you had been in David's situation? What do you think you would have been feeling?

Read Psalm 3

DICTIONARY

Selah (v 2,4,8): probably a musical instruction.
Deliverance (v 8): rescue.

4. Psalm 3 was written when David fled from Absalom. How did David sleep that night?

5. David says: "I will not fear" (v 6). What enables him to respond to the situation without fear?

6. Look at verse 3. What normally is the shield of a king? What is the glory of a king? What is the position of a king?

7. David has lost his army, his glory and his exalted position. But what has he *not* lost?

8. How does this enable David to respond?

David does not fear the future because he values God more than anything on earth, and nothing can take God away from him.

apply

David says: "I will not fear..." He does not say: "I do not fear..." He decides not to fear. He tells himself not to fear. It is an act of will based on the truth of God's word. He "preaches" the truth to himself so that he will not fear.

9. How do people deal with anxiety? How about you?

10. How can we learn to "preach the truth" to ourselves so that we do not fear?

getting personal

Think about situations in which you fear the loss of protection (your shield), pleasure (your glory) or your reputation (your exalted position). How would trust and delight in God transform your fears?

explore more

optional

Look at verses 7-8. The deliverance of David = the blessing of God's people. David points to Jesus. Jesus is David's greater Son. David was anointed king over God's people and Jesus is the anointed King of God's people (the word "Christ" = anointed one).

How is the deliverance described in verse 7 fulfilled in Jesus?
How does the deliverance of Jesus bring blessing to God's people?
How can these truths help us cope with anxious nights?

11. Here is an "anti-psalm" of Psalm 3. The song has been rewritten to make it say the opposite of what it actually says.

I've got so many problems!
It seems as if everyone's against me.
Everyone says: "You have to look after number one".
My security is in my bank balance,
I glory in my possessions,
I want to rise up the career ladder.
I complain to anyone who'll hear me.
I lie awake at night
and in the morning I'm worn out with worry.
I'm worried about all the people who get in my way.
I need to get up; I need to get going.
I need to beat the opposition.
I need to show them who's best.
My success comes through my hard work.
I'm going to make sure I enjoy the good life.

Which of the statements in this anti-psalm sound like things you might say or think?

- Work out what the corresponding line is in the real psalm. How do these truths set us free us from worry?

investigate

Read Psalm 4

Again we see David sleeping well (v 8). Here the focus is on angry nights (v 4). David imagines someone lying in bed at night, brooding over how they have been wronged, replaying events and conversations in their mind—frustrated, bitter or fuming.

DICTIONARY

Delusions (v 2): beliefs which are completely wrong.
Grain and new wine (v 7): a picture of having plenty of possessions.

12. Look at verses 1-3. We often get angry because our reputation is at stake. What is David's response?

13. Look at verses 4-5.
What is David's prescription when anger keeps us awake at night?

14. Why does David invite us to search our hearts? See James 4 v 1.

Sometimes we get angry because we are concerned for God's glory or because we love other people. Jesus himself was sometimes angry. But more often we get angry because of self-centred desires in our hearts. We get angry when those desires are threatened or frustrated, and when we are not getting our way.

getting personal

Think about the last time you got angry—perhaps even brooded about it at night. What triggered your anger? Anger is a sign that we are not getting what we want. What desires in your heart does your anger reveal?

apply

15. Look at verses 6-8.
What is David's remedy for self-centred desires?

- How could we put this remedy into practice?

pray

Look at what David says about God and his relationship with God in these two songs. Use this as a basis of praise to God.

List some things you are anxious or angry about. Ask God to help you to remove your anxiety and anger as you delight in him.

2

Psalm 16

A SONG FOR WHEN SIN SEEMS GOOD

talkabout

1. When do we find sin attractive? What are some of the sinful things we might want to do because they seem pleasurable?

investigate

Read 1 Samuel 26

2. What temptations did David face?

DICTIONARY

Saul (v 1): King of Israel before David. At this point, God has chosen David as the next king, so Saul's trying to kill him.
Lord's anointed (v 9,11,23): a king chosen by God to rule his people, shown by oil being poured on his head.

Read Psalm 16

It's quite possible that the events of 1 Samuel 26, where David is taunted and told to follow other gods, are the situation in which this was written.

3. Look at verses 1-2. How does David respond to the attraction of sinning in this stressful situation?

DICTIONARY

Holy people / Saints (v 3): Distinctive people ie: people who follow God.
Libations (v 4): a drink poured out as an offering to a god.
Lot (v 5): an amount given to someone.

4. Look at verses 3-4. What does David say about God's people?

5. What does David say about those who live for other gods?

apply

6. How does the community of God's people help us when sin seems good?

getting personal

Other Christians can only help us walk with God if we have relationships of openness and grace, in which people know us well and feel free to rebuke us. Do you have relationships like this? Are you willing both to be challenged and to challenge other Christians?

investigate

7. What is the "delightful inheritance" (NIV) David talks about in verse 6? (Note: the ESV translation for v 5a is better: "The LORD is my chosen portion and my cup".)

8. In 1 Samuel 26 David says: "They have driven me today from my share in the LORD's inheritance and have said, 'Go, serve other gods.'" (v 19) What is David's response in this psalm?

9. Look at verses 7-8. What truths about God does David celebrate in these verses?

10. Look at verses 8-11 and Acts 2 v 22-32. How does Peter say that Psalm 16 is fulfilled?

David said: "You will not abandon me to the grave / realm of the dead". Jesus can say: "You did not abandon me to the grave". Christians are in Christ—he is our representative. So we can now say: "You will not abandon us to the grave".

11. How does the victory of Jesus help us when sin seems good?

When the pleasures of sin shine bright, we should respond by saying to God: "You are my Lord" (repentance and obedience) and "apart from you I have no good thing" (faith).

This psalm identifies four things to remember that will help us do this:

1. The community of other Christians (v 3-4)
2. The goodness of God the Father (v 5-6)
3. The presence of God the Spirit (v 7-8)
4. The victory of God the Son (v 9-11)

apply

12. Sometimes we are tempted because sin seems attractive. Sometimes we are tempted because sin seems inevitable. How do the goodness, the presence and the victory of God help us when we face temptation?

13. David says: "I keep my eyes always on the LORD" (v 8). Think of some practical things we can do to put the Lord in our line of sight when sin seems good.

pray

Use these headings to thank God and ask for his help in your struggle with temptation:

1. The community of other Christians (v 3-4)
2. The goodness of God the Father (v 5-6)
3. The presence of God the Spirit (v 7-8)
4. The victory of God the Son (v 9-11)

3 Psalm 18

A SONG FOR WHEN WE WANT TO RUN AWAY

talkabout

1. When do you feel like running away?

2. What are some of the ways you escape pressure?

We all have times when we would like to run away from the pressures that face us. It might be a daunting task, a difficult relationship or a lonely evening. Some people escape by creating moments of pleasure. Eating chocolate cake or playing computer solitaire takes our mind off things. But it does not make the problems go away. Other people create a fantasy world in which they are strong or adored. But, whether they are romantic, sexual or success fantasies, they are still just fantasies—they are not reality.

getting personal

What are you trying to escape from at the moment?

Can you imagine being able to face up to this situation instead?

How willing are you to look to God to help you in this, as you learn from this psalm?

investigate

Psalm 18 ends with the words: "[God] gives his king great victories; he shows unfailing love to his anointed, to David and his descendants for ever." David was God's anointed king. This psalm is about David and his descendants. And David's greatest descendant is Jesus Christ (the word "Christ" means "anointed one"). So this is actually a psalm about Jesus. And so we who are "in Christ" can read this psalm as applying to us also.

Read Psalm 18 v 1-6

DICTIONARY

Horn (v 2): a symbol of strength.
Snares (v 5): traps.
Temple (v 6): in this context, heaven—the place God dwells in all his fulness.

3. Look at the inscription (the introduction before v 1). What pressures was David facing? How are these reflected in the psalm (see v 4-6 especially)?

4. Where does David turn when he feels overwhelmed?

getting personal

Look at the way David keeps saying "my" in verses 1-3. We too can say: "God is my strength… my rock… my fortress… my deliverer… my refuge… my shield… my salvation… my stronghold".

Pick the description of God that you need most at the moment, and turn it into prayer or praise.

Read Psalm 18 v 6-15

DICTIONARY

Cherubim (v 10): angels.
Routed (v 14): completely defeated someone.
Rebuke (v 15): strong telling-off.

5. How does God respond to David's cry for help?

6. How does David describe God?

Read Psalm 18 v 16-19

7. What does this thundering, fire-breathing, earth-shattering God do when he arrives?

getting personal

Who are the people or problems that make you feel like running away? In your imagination, put them side by side with God as he is described in these verses. How do they look when placed next to God?

Read Psalm 18 v 20-27

8. How do you react when you read these words? Why?

DICTIONARY

Righteousness (v 20, 24): in this context, living the right way, God's way.
Decrees (v 22): commands.
The humble (v 27): people who don't think more highly of themselves than they should.
Haughty (v 27): people who think of themselves more highly than they should.

apply

9. Remember this psalm is about Jesus (v 50). Read v 20-27 as a description of Jesus. And then read them as a description of us, clothed in Christ's righteousness. What does this show about how the Lord deals with us?

investigate

10. What does it mean for God to be faithful towards us? Blameless towards us? Pure towards us?

Read Psalm 18 v 28-36

11. How do you feel when you are overwhelmed or under pressure? How does David feel when he makes God his refuge?

Read Psalm 18 v 37-50

12. David describes the victory God will give his anointed king. How are these verses fulfilled in Jesus Christ?

DICTIONARY

Adversaries (v 39): enemies.
Exalted (v 48): publicly raised up.

apply

13. How does the truth of Christ's victory help us when we feel like running away?

14. What are you going to do next time you feel like running away?

pray

Talk about some of the ways in which you feel overwhelmed, or situations in which you want to run away. Turn Psalm 18 into prayer.

Verses 1-5	Give thanks that God is our rock, fortress, deliverer, refuge and so on.
Verses 6-19	Cry out to God to help you in your specific situation. Ask him to come in power, reach down from on high and lift you up into a spacious place.
Verses 20-27	Confess your sin and fear, and thank God that he treats you as righteous in Christ.
Verses 28-36	Ask God for the strength and courage to face your problems through trust in him.
Verses 37-50	Give thanks for the victory of Jesus and ask God to deliver you from your enemies.

4 Psalm 23
A SONG FOR DARK DAYS

talkabout

1. Think about a dark time in your life. How did you find comfort in your situation?

David says: "I will fear no evil". This is a psalm of calm confidence, even though it is a psalm to be sung in "the valley of the shadow of death" or "darkest valley". That confidence comes from David's knowledge of God and his relationship with God.

investigate

Read Psalm 23 v 1-4

2. What does God do for David?

3. David uses the picture of a shepherd caring for his sheep to describe God. Rewrite verses 1-4 using an image from our day.

4. What do you think David meant by "the valley of the shadow of death" or "the darkest valley"? What does this picture suggest to you?

apply

5. How can we experience the blessings of verses 1-3 when we are going through the darkness of verse 4?

getting personal

Think back to the last time you had a dark day. What made it a dark day? How did you respond? Did you turn to God for comfort? Did verses 1-4 describe how you felt?

explore more

optional

David says: "Your rod and your staff, they comfort me" (v 4).

Read Exodus 14 v 13-31 and 17 v 1-7

What did the staff of God do for his people?

Exodus says that the staff that struck the rock was the same staff that struck the Nile in judgment.

Read 1 Corinthians 10 v 4

How does this verse help us see the bigger picture of what is being shown here?

What did it mean for David to find comfort in God's rod and staff?

What does it mean for us?

explore more

optional

Read Ezekiel 34 v 1-24

Who are the shepherds of Israel?

What is the problem with them?

What does God promise to do in response?

Through whom will God fulfil this promise (compare v 11 with v 23)?

investigate

Read John 10 v 7-16

6. What blessings does Jesus, the good Shepherd, provide for his people?

- How does He provide them?

- How do we receive them?

apply

7. How can we find comfort in Jesus, the good Shepherd, when we have dark days?

investigate

Read Psalm 23 v 5-6

8. In verses 5-6 the picture changes from God as our shepherd to God as our host. Rewrite verses 5-6 with an image from our day.

9. What does it mean for goodness and love to follow us? What does it mean for goodness and mercy to follow us into the valley of darkness?

Read Romans 8 v 28-39

10. How do these verses expand our understanding of Psalm 23 v 5-6?
- What does Paul say about God's goodness?

- What is "the good" that God works for us?

- What are our enemies, and how does God bless us in the face of these enemies?

- How does Paul express David's conviction that we "will dwell in the house of the LORD for ever"?

apply

11. Psalm 23 expresses calm confidence in the face of a dark situation. Where does David get this confidence from? How can we imitate him?

12. Think of some practical ways in which we can live our lives "in the house of the LORD".

getting personal

Imagine a house in which God has prepared a feast for you. He will honour you as his guest ("anointing your head") and your cup will overflow as you find true satisfaction. And God's feast is free because Jesus has paid the price (Isaiah 55 v 1-2).

Now imagine another house in which sin invites you to dine. It entices you with promises of satisfaction, but those promises are lies because it does not truly satisfy. And the price tag is "death" (Romans 6 v 23).

In which house are you going to eat today?

pray

Praise God...

- for spiritual and physical provision from God in this life.
- for spiritual and physical provision from God for the life to come.

Pray to God...

- for people you know going through the valley of darkness.

Count the times that David says "I" or "my" or "me" in Psalm 23. Ask God to make the truths in the psalm personal to you.

5 Psalm 27
A SONG FOR WHEN WE ARE AFRAID

talkabout

1. What are you afraid of?

investigate

Read Psalm 27

DICTIONARY

Tabernacle / sacred tent (v 5): the tent in Israel where God was particularly present among his people..
Forsake (v 9,10): abandon, turn your back on.

2. What can we know about David's situation from the psalm?

3. Look at verses 1-6. Who is David speaking to, do you think?

4. Look at verses 1-3. What does David feel in this situation?

5. What is the reason for David's confidence?

6. Look at verses 4-6. What is the one big thing that David seeks?

apply

7. We are often afraid because we are worried about what we might lose. How does knowing God help us overcome this fear?

8. We are often afraid because of what might happen to us. How does knowing God help us overcome this fear?

9. David begins this psalm by talking to himself. What should we tell ourselves when we are afraid?

getting personal

Think about situations when you fear losing something (your job, someone you love). Think about situations when you fear what might happen to you. Pick a line from verses 1-6 that specifically applies to those situations.

investigate

10. Look at verses 7-12. Who is David talking to in these verses?

11. What does David say about God in verses 7-12?

12. What does David ask God in verses 7-12?

apply

13. How should we pray when we feel afraid?

investigate

14. One of the things we often fear is rejection. We worry about what other people think of us. We "need" their approval. Look at verses 8-10. What answer does David give for this kind of fear?

15. How does fear affect our behaviour?
Why does David pray as he does in verse 11?

16. Look at verses 13-14. What should we do when we are afraid?

apply

17. How can we help one another overcome our fear?

pray

Use verses 7-12 as the basis for your prayers. Think of fears you face or people you know. Read out Psalm 27 one verse at a time and then turn it into prayer for these situations.

6 Psalm 32

A SONG FOR SECRET GUILT

talkabout

1. What attitude do people in general have towards sin?

2. What do people say we should do if we feel guilty?

investigate

Read Psalm 32

3. Look at verses 1-2. How does David define blessing?

DICTIONARY

Transgressions (v 1,5): another word for sins.
Sapped (v 4): drained.
Iniquity (v 5): wrongdoing.
Counsel (v 8): advise.
RIghteous (v 11): those who are right with God through trusting in his promises and seeking to live his way.

4. Who does God bless?

5. Look at verses 3-5. What was David silent about?

6. What happens when we deny or hide our sin?

7. What happens when we confess our sin to the LORD?

explore more

optional

Read Psalm 38

What effect does sin have on David?

How does David respond to the situation he is in (see verses 18 and 21-22)?

How does God discipline us today?

Is sickness always a result of God's discipline?

apply

8. In what ways do we try to deny or hide our sin?

9. What consequences have you seen in individuals when they have tried to deny or hide their sin? What consequences do we see in society when people try to ignore the reality of sin?

getting personal

Are there ways in which you deny your sin? Perhaps you blame other people or your circumstances. Perhaps you pretend it's not too serious.

Are there ways in which you hide your sin? Is there sin you have not confessed to other people? Is there sin you have not confessed to God?

What have been the consequences in your life?

investigate

10. Look at verses 6-7. What is David's remedy for the problem of secret sin?

11. David says that God will protect us if we confess our sin. How does confession lead to protection? From what are we protected?

explore more

optional

What Bible story involves "mighty waters" that "rise" (verse 6)?

What were the rising waters a sign or consequence of in the story?

How do we escape the rising waters?

12. Look at verses 8-11. What advice does David give to us?

13. How can we be like a stubborn mule (v 9)?

apply

14. Is it good to feel guilty? Should we encourage people to feel guilty?

15. How do we hide sin in the church?
What effect does this have on the Christian community?

16. What value is there in confessing our sin to another person?

pray

If we claim to have fellowship with him and yet walk in the darkness, we lie and do not live out the truth. But if we walk in the light, as he is in the light, we have fellowship with one another, and the blood of Jesus, his Son, purifies us from all sin. If we claim to be without sin, we deceive ourselves and the truth is not in us (1 John 1 v 6-8).

Spend some time in quiet reflection. Is there secret sin in your life? What are its consequences? What are you missing out on?

If we confess our sins, he is faithful and just and will forgive us our sins and purify us from all unrighteousness (1 John 1 v 9).

Spend some time silently or openly confessing your sin.

If anybody does sin, we have an advocate with the Father—Jesus Christ, the Righteous One. He is the atoning sacrifice for our sins, and not only for ours but also for the sins of the whole world (1 John 2 v 1-2).

Spend some time giving thanks to God for his forgiveness. Give thanks for Jesus, who bore God's anger against sin on the cross in our place.

Rejoice in the LORD and be glad, you righteous; sing, all you who are upright in heart! (Psalm 32 v 11).

Soul songs: Leader's Guide

INTRODUCTION

Leading a Bible study can be a bit like herding cats—everyone has a different idea of what the passage could be about, and a different line of enquiry that they want to pursue. But a good group leader is more than someone who just referees this kind of discussion. You will want to:

- correctly understand and handle the Bible passage. But also...
- encourage and train the people in your group to do this for themselves. Don't fall into the trap of spoon-feeding people by simply passing on the information in the Leader's Guide. Then...
- make sure that no Bible study is finished without everyone knowing how the passage is relevant for them. What changes do you all need to make in the light of the things you have been learning? And finally...
- encourage the group to turn all that has been learned and discussed into prayer.

Your Bible-study group is unique, and you are likely to know better than anyone the capabilities, backgrounds and circumstances of the people you are leading. That's why we've designed these guides with a number of optional features. If they're a quiet bunch, you might want to spend longer on talkabout. If your time is limited, you can choose to skip explore more, or get people to look at these questions at home. Can't get enough of Bible study? Well, some studies have optional extra homework projects. As leader, you can adapt and select the material to the needs of your particular group.

So what's in the Leader's Guide? The main thing that this Leader's Guide will help you to do is to understand the major teaching points in the passage you are studying, and how to apply them. As well as guidance on the questions, the Leader's Guide for each session contains the following important sections:

THE BIG IDEA

One key sentence will give you the main point of the session. This is what you should be aiming to have fixed in people's minds as they leave the Bible study. And it's the point you need to head back towards when the discussion goes off at a tangent.

SUMMARY

An overview of the passage, including plenty of useful historical background information.

OPTIONAL EXTRA

Usually this is an introductory activity that ties in with the main theme of the Bible study, and is designed to "break the ice" at the beginning of a session. Or it may be a "homework project" that people can tackle during the week.

So let's take a look at the various different features of a Good Book Guide:

talkabout

Each session kicks off with a discussion question, based on the group's opinions or experiences. It's designed to get people talking and thinking in a general way about the main subject of the Bible study.

investigate

The first thing you and your group need to know is what the Bible passage is about, which is the purpose of these questions. But watch out—people may come up with answers based on their experiences or teaching they have heard in the past, without referring to the passage at all. It's amazing how often we can get through a Bible study without actually looking at the Bible! If you're stuck for an answer, the Leader's Guide contains guidance on questions. These are the answers to direct your group to. This information isn't meant to be read out to people—ideally, you want them to discover these answers from the Bible for themselves. Sometimes there are optional follow-up questions (see in guidance on questions) to help you help your group get to the answer.

explore more

These questions generally point people to other relevant parts of the Bible. They are useful for helping your group to see how the passage fits into the "big picture" of the whole Bible. These sections are OPTIONAL—only use them if you have time. Remember that it's better to finish in good time having really grasped one big thing from the passage, than to try and cram everything in.

apply

We want to encourage you to spend more time working at application—too often, it is simply tacked on at the end. In the Good Book Guides, apply sections are mixed in with the investigate sections of the study. We hope that people will realise that application is not just an optional extra, but rather, the whole purpose of studying the Bible. We do Bible study so that our lives can be changed by what we hear from God's word. If you skip the application, the Bible study hasn't achieved its purpose.

These questions draw out practical lessons that we can all learn from the Bible passage. You can review what has been learned so far, and think about practical differences that this should make in our churches and our lives. The group gets the opportunity to talk about what they personally have learned.

getting personal

These can be done at home, but it is well worth allowing a few moments of quiet reflection during the study for each person to think and pray about specific changes they need to make in their own lives. Why not have a time for reporting back at the beginning of the following session, so that everyone can be encouraged and challenged by one another to make application a priority?

pray

In Acts 4 v 25-30 the first Christians quoted Psalm 2 as they prayed in response to the persecution of the apostles by the Jewish religious leaders. Today however, it's not as common for Christians to base prayers on the truths of God's word as it once was. As a result, our prayers tend to be weak, superficial and self-centred rather than bold, visionary and God-centred.

The prayer section is based on what has been learned from the Bible passage. How different our prayer times would be if we were genuinely responding to what God has said to us through his word.

1

Psalms 3 and 4

A SONG FOR SLEEPLESS NIGHTS

THE BIG IDEA

Delight in God is the answer to the worries and bitterness that keep us awake at night, brooding.

SUMMARY

Psalm 3 was written when David fled from a coup led by his son Absalom. We might have thought he would be full of anxiety and anger. We can imagine him lying awake on that first night, brooding with fear about the future, and anger about the past. But in both Psalm 3 and Psalm 4, David says he can sleep well (3 v 5 and 4 v 8). David is not consumed with fear or anger because his delight is in God. God matters more to David than his earthly power and privilege. He is not fearful because nothing can separate him from God: "You, Lord, are a shield around me, my glory, the One who lifts my head high" (3 v 3). And he is not angry because his delight is in God: "Fill my heart with joy when their grain and new wine abound" (4 v 7).

GUIDANCE FOR QUESTIONS

1. What thoughts or feelings keep you awake at night? Two common reasons are anxiety and anger. We lie awake worrying about the future. We turn over "what ifs" in our heads. Or we replay incidents that have made us angry or frustrated. We compose responses in our heads.

- **Imagine you are lying awake at night because you are brooding on something. What thoughts or feelings are going through your head?**

2. What is David's situation? He is fleeing from a rebellion led by his son, Absalom, which looks as though it will be successful.

3. What do you think you would have been thinking if you had been in David's situation? What do you think you would have been feeling? Highlight the fact that David seems to have had good reasons to feel anxious about the future and angry about the past.

4. Psalm 3 was written when David fled from Absalom. How did David sleep that night? He slept well! (v 5).

5. David says: "I will not fear" (v 6). What enables him to respond to the situation without fear? Emphasise the connection between David's intimate knowledge of and trust in God, and his astonishing lack of fear. How well we know and trust God really does make a difference to how we feel in times of trouble!

6. Look at verse 3. What normally is the shield of a king? What is the glory of a king? What is the position of a king? The "shield" of a king is his army. The glory of a king is his throne and his court. And a king has the top position in society.

7. David has lost his army, his glory and his exalted position. But what has he not lost? His relationship with God.

8. How does this enable David to respond? God is his shield and glory. God is the one who honours David by lifting him up. This matters more to David than the earthly trappings of power and privilege. He is confident about the future not because he believes God will definitely restore him to the throne, but because no one can take from him that which he values most—his relationship with God. See Romans 8 v 31-39.

9 and 10. APPLY: How do people deal with anxiety? How about you? How can we learn to "preach the truth" to ourselves so that we do not fear? Be aware that these application questions may bring up some difficult issues. When people have not been sleeping well, either through worry or anger, then they will tend to be more irritable and sensitive to these issues. Ironically, lack of sleep through thinking these things over can make people less able to cope with the realities they are struggling with. There may also be people who struggle with sleeping at night for purely medical reasons. Make sure that you don't place any additional burden on them by suggesting that the problem is a lack of trust in the Lord. It may be appropriate to encourage people to seek medical help if this is a problem.

EXPLORE MORE

How is the deliverance described in verse 7 fulfilled in Jesus? How does the deliverance of Jesus bring blessing to God's people? How can these truths help us cope with anxious nights? Jesus delivered us from sin through his death. God's people (those who trust in Christ) have the sure hope of eternal life. We can fight anxiety by remembering that our future is secure.

11. Which of the statements in this anti-psalm sound like things you might say or think? See Study Guide, page 10.

- **Work out what the corresponding line is in the real psalm. How do these truths set us free us from worry?** Give your group plenty of time and encourage them to be honest and personal in their answers.

12. Look at verses 1-3. We often get angry because our reputation is at stake. What is David's response? He looks to God to sort it out for him.

- **Look at 1 Peter 2 v 18-25. How did Jesus respond when his reputation was on the line (v 23)?**

13. Look at verses 4-5. What is David's prescription when anger keeps us awake at night? He tells us to search our hearts, to stop fuming or replaying conversations ("be silent"), to plan to look to God instead of planning revenge and trust God to vindicate us. The mention of self-searching and sacrifice in these two verses should raise the issue of our own sinfulness, our need for forgiveness and our ineligibility to judge those who have wronged us. As believers, we can look to the righteous sacrifice that Jesus made on our behalf on the cross. We can rest on that, knowing that, even though our sinful hearts may accuse us, it has all been dealt with in his death for us.

14. Why does David invite us to search our hearts? See James 4 v 1. The source of anger is not our circumstances ("I was angry because he said..."). Circumstances are just the trigger. The source of anger is the desires within us. Sometimes those desires are bad; sometimes they are good desires that have grown more important to us than knowing and serving God ("I was angry because I want to be treated with respect"). Anger is a sign that our desires are frustrated in some way—that we are not getting what we want.

- **What does James say is the real cause of our anger?**

15. APPLY: Look at v 6-8. What is David's remedy for self-centred desires? Our desires are battling with the Holy Spirit for control of our hearts (Galatians 5 v 16-17). David had every reason to be angry, but instead he delighted in God. So lying awake at night is an opportunity to get our hearts right with God through repentance (see James 4 v 4-10).

- **How could we put this remedy into practice?** Encourage your group to make practical suggestions for their own lives.

OPTIONAL EXTRA

Ask people to write their own "anti-psalm" for Psalm 4. This is an exercise that you can use with any of these studies on the psalms. This encourages people to look at the text in detail. It also helps them see what happens in our lives when we do not live out the truths of the psalm.
Look at some statistics on sleep and sleeplessness. Use them to create a short quiz. Look up some websites on insomnia to get some background, and offer some practical help and tips to those who are struggling with sleep issues.
Pastoral note: For any of your group who do struggle with sleep, the temptation to think about their own worries in the middle of the night can exacerbate the problem. Why not suggest that they spend the time praying for others if they find themselves awake at night.

---

2 Psalm 16
A SONG FOR WHEN SIN SEEMS GOOD

THE BIG IDEA

The goodness of God and the help of God enable us to overcome temptation.

SUMMARY

We cannot be sure about the context of this psalm, but it seems David was fleeing for refuge (v 1). We do not know what "miktam" in the inscription means, though it resembles the word for "cover". Four of the six psalms with this inscription refer to specific events in David's life, and three of those refer to his years as an outlaw. So miktam psalms might be songs of covering or refuge. In 1 Samuel 26 David enters Saul's camp and steals some of his personal effects, but does not kill him. Then David proclaims his loyalty to Saul and complains: "They have now driven me from my share in the LORD's inheritance and have said, 'Go, serve other gods.'" (1 Samuel 26 v 19) In Psalm 16 he refuses to serve other gods (verse 4) and affirms his delight in the LORD's inheritance (verses 5-6). So it seems likely that Psalm 16 was written during David's years as a fugitive.

When sin seems good, we should respond as David does in verse 2, by saying to God: "You are my Lord" (repentance and obedience) and "apart from you I have no good thing" (faith). This psalm identifies four things to remember that will help us do this:
1. The community of other Christians (v 3-4)
2. The goodness of God the Father (v 5-6)
3. The presence of God the Spirit (v 7-8)
4. The victory of God the Son (v 9-11)

GUIDANCE FOR QUESTIONS

1. When do we find sin attractive? What are some of the sinful things we might want to do because they seem pleasurable? The Puritan preacher, Richard Baxter, said: "The will never desires evil as evil but as ... seeming good" (*A Christian Directory*). Highlight the fact that when we face temptation, sin rarely seems like a bad or evil thing. It always looks attractive to us at the time. Humanity's first sin illustrates this: "When the woman saw that the fruit of the tree was good for food and pleasing to the eye, and also desirable for gaining wisdom, she took some and ate it" (Genesis 3 v 6).

2. (In 1 Samuel 26) What temptations did David face? Probably to take revenge or to despair. People also encouraged him to serve other gods (1 Samuel 26 v 19) and to give up on God's people.

3. Look at verses 1-2. How does David respond to the attraction of sinning in this stressful situation? He is fearful of sin, and seems to understand its power to corrupt him. He calls on God to preserve him and runs away from it to the Lord, his hiding place (refuge). He has a refuge from physical danger, but he understands that sin is just as dangerous as the army that is hunting him down (if not more!). He has a long-term view of sin, and sees that all the pleasures of sin end in ruin and judgment. This is how he can say: "Apart from you I have no good thing".

4. Look at verses 3-4. What does David say about God's people? He takes delight in them. True glory is found among God's people. Note that "holy people" or "saints" are not super-spiritual people, but anyone who is a follower of the Lord. We may be inspired by the lives of great Christians from the past, but our delight comes from thinking about our "ordinary" brothers and sisters in Christ.

5. What does David say about those who live for other gods? David will not join in the sinful activities of unbelievers. He recognises that their activities will eventually result in sorrow. See also **Psalm 1**.

6. APPLY: How does the community of God's people help us when sin seems good? Other Christians can encourage and challenge us. They can hold us accountable and keep us from situations in which temptation is strong for us. They remind us that true delight is found in knowing and serving God (v 3 and 6).

7. What is the "delightful inheritance" (NIV) David talks about in verse 6? The imagery in verse 6 is that of an inheritance in the promised land. But in verse 5 David says: "LORD, you alone are my chosen portion and my cup". God himself is David's inheritance.

8. In 1 Samuel 26 David says: "They have driven me today from my share in the LORD's inheritance and have said,

'Go, serve other gods.'" (v 19) What is David's response in this psalm?
"Driven me from my share in the LORD's inheritance" = driven out of the promised land (see Deuteronomy 20 v 16; 32 v 9). David responds by asserting that God himself is his inheritance. He may not enjoy the blessings of the land, but he does find delight in God. And so he will not serve other "gods", who do not satisfy.

9. Look at v 7-8. What truths about God does David celebrate in these verses?
He is with us to guide (v 7) and help us (v 8).

- **How are these things true for Christians?** See John 14 v 16; 1 Corinthians 2 v 12-16; Philippians 1 v 19; 2 Timothy 1 v 14. Christians recognise that this is the work of the Holy Spirit within them.

10. Look at verses 8-11 and Acts 2 v 22-32. How does Peter say that Psalm 16 is fulfilled? Psalm 16 describes David's experience. But David was a pointer to Jesus. Jesus is God's anointed King and David's greater Son. So this song is fulfilled in the resurrection of Jesus: "Seeing what was to come, [David] spoke of the resurrection of the Messiah, that he was not abandoned to the realm of the dead [or "grave"], nor did his body see decay" (Acts 2 v 31).

11. How does the victory of Jesus help us when sin seems good? The struggle with sin is temporary—it is only for this life. And we will not be defeated. Sin cannot overcome those who trust in Christ.

12. APPLY: How do the goodness, the presence and the victory of God help us when we face temptation?
- God's *goodness*: Finding delight in God makes sin less attractive because we realise only God truly satisfies.
- God's *presence*: Remembering the presence of God helps us realise sin is not inevitable. God can help us overcome temptation. "With him at my right hand, I will not be shaken" (v 8).
- God's *victory*: It is not inevitable that we will sin because Jesus has broken sin's power, through his death and resurrection.

13. APPLY: David says: "I keep my eyes always on the LORD" (v 8). Think of some practical things we can do to put the Lord in our line of sight when sin seems good. These ideas might include things like sticking up Bible verses round the home or over our desk at work, phoning a friend for encouragement, listening to Christian music in the car, memorising Bible verses and so on. Encourage people to share things they do already.

OPTIONAL EXTRA

In Psalm 16 David is not giving advice on coping with temptation. He actually is coping with temptation by reminding himself of God's goodness and help. He is keeping his eyes on the Lord (v 8). As a group, write your own psalm, in which you remind yourself why obedience and faith in God are better than the pleasures of sin.

Pastoral note: Be aware that this study may bring up some sin issues with group members. The hardest sins for us to deal with are those that we enjoy doing—be that gossiping, hoarding money (lack of generosity), or pride in our achievements or status. A good place to start dealing with these is your own honesty in talking about the things you struggle with.

3 Psalm 18

A SONG FOR WHEN WE WANT TO RUN AWAY

THE BIG IDEA

When we feel we want to run away from our pressures, we should run to God.

SUMMARY

It may not appear obvious at first sight, but this psalm is actually all about Christ (see v 50). David was God's anointed king. This psalm is about David and his descendants. And David's greatest descendant is Jesus Christ (the word "Christ" means "anointed one"). So this is actually a psalm about Jesus. And so Christians, who are "in Christ", can read this psalm as applying to us also. When we want to run away, we should turn to God as our refuge or our place of escape (v 1-5). He is the awesome God (v 6-15), who comes to rescue us (v 16-19). We are righteous through Christ (v 20-27). He gives us strength to cope with adversity (v 28-36) and we share his victory (v 37-50).

We all have different ways of escaping the pressures of life—everything from eating chocolate cake to creating sexual fantasies. When we feel we want to run away from our pressures, we should run to God as David does in this psalm.

GUIDANCE FOR QUESTIONS

1-2. When do you feel like running away? What are some of the ways you escape pressure? Keep careful note of the answers to these questions. They will undoubtedly bring up some concerns that you will want to pray through at the end of the session.

3. Look at the inscription (the introduction before v 1). What pressures was David facing? How are these reflected in the psalm (see v 4-6 especially)? He was in fear of death. In fact, he thought he was a goner. There seemed to be absolutely no hope that he would come out of it with his life.

4. Where does David turn when he feels overwhelmed? He finds refuge in God his rock, his fortress and his deliverer.

- **Note David's description of God in v 1-3. How do you imagine he feels, compared with the experiences of v 4-6?**

5. How does God respond to David's cry for help? He comes in power and glory to help David.

- **How does God feel? Why?** Angry (v 7). He feels this way because his people are precious to him—see Deuteronomy 32 v 9-10.
- **How personal is God's involvement in David's rescue?** God doesn't send angels—he himself acts. Note v 9 and its parallel with the Lord Jesus Christ in John 6 v 42.
- **What is the effect of God's intervention?** Nothing can resist him.

6. How does David describe God? Encourage people to rephrase some of these images in their own words.

7. What does this thundering, fire-breathing, earth-shattering God do when he arrives? Draw out the contrast between the majesty of God and the tender way he cares for his people.

8. How do you react when you read these words (v 20-27)? Why? People may feel overwhelmed or condemned because they know that they have not lived like this, and cannot do it. Others may read them as a description of Christ's righteousness because they know that sinners can only become sinless in God's eyes if they are "in Christ" (see 1 Corinthians 1 v 30 and Hebrews 10 v 14). Depending on your group, it may be that no one will read verses 20-24 as a description of Jesus Christ, in which case you can use this follow-up question to raise the issue:

- **Compare David's words about himself, written in Psalm 51 v 1-5. How do you think both psalms could be true?**

9. APPLY: Remember this psalm is about Jesus (v 50). Read v 20-27 as a description of Jesus. And then read them as a description of us, clothed in Christ's righteousness. What does this show about how the Lord deals with us? The Lord has dealt with us according to Christ's righteousness; according to the cleanness of Christ's hands he has rewarded us. In Christ, God shows himself to us as faithful, blameless and pure.
Some may query why verses 20-27 are interpreted as being about Christ's righteousness, when David seems clearly to be writing about his own righteousness. It is important to establish the following points:
A: A comparison with other psalms written by David (eg: Psalm 51) will show that he certainly did not believe he was perfect.
B: From the way in which David's psalms are quoted and used in the New Testament, we know that (knowingly or unknowingly) he was a prophetic writer. Things that he wrote about himself later came to be also true (but in a greater and more significant way) of Jesus Christ. Eg: Psalm 16 v 8-11, quoted in Acts 2 v 25-28.
In the light of these two factors, the options for deciding how to understand v 20-24 are:
i) David deduces, from the rewards and favour he has received from God, that God must consider him blameless, although he doesn't know how this can be (since he is well aware of his sin). We, however, with the help of the New Testament, can see that David was made blameless by Christ's sacrificial death on the cross. Romans 3 v 25 tells us that Jesus' death paid for the sins of those who had lived in earlier times.
ii) David knows somehow about God's plan of salvation, to be carried out in the future when Christ dies. He knows God will consider him blameless through his faith in what Christ is going to do, so he writes this as an expression of confidence and celebration in what Christ will do for him.
Whether David knew about the future work of Christ or not when he wrote this psalm, the NT is clear that no one is without sin, but all can be made perfect in Christ (see Romans 3 v 10-24).
Note: If all this is new to people in the group, this would be a good opportunity to make sure that everyone knows the basic facts of the gospel and what a Christian is.

10. What does it mean for God to be faithful towards us? Blameless towards us? Pure towards us? God's dealings with us are faithful—he keeps his promises to us. His dealings with us are blameless—when we look back from eternity we will not be able to fault them. And his dealings with us are pure—they are without any malice.

11. How do you feel when you are overwhelmed or under pressure? How does David feel when he makes God his refuge? Highlight the energy and confidence that David has when God is his refuge. "I can advance against a troop … I can scale a wall … God arms me with strength … He makes my feet like the feet of a deer."

12. David describes the victory God will give his anointed king. How are these verses fulfilled in Jesus Christ?

- **What or who are the enemies of Jesus? What or who are our enemies? How are they defeated by Jesus?** Jesus defeats sin, fear, death and Satan through the cross and resurrection.

13. APPLY: How does the truth of Christ's victory help us when we feel like running away? We will go through many ups and downs in life. But we can be confident that we will share in Christ's victory. God will bring us safely home to eternal life. Sin and death will not have the last word. See 1 Corinthians 15 v 54-58.

14. APPLY: What are you going to do next time you feel like running away? An opportunity both to summarise what we have seen in Psalm 18 and to apply it in practical ways. The heart of people's answer to this question should be to trust in God's care over us and look to him for refuge. But it might be helpful to think of some ways in which people can remind themselves of this truth when they are tempted to look elsewhere for refuge. Someone, for example, might stick verse 2 on their biscuit tin or next to their computer screen.

---

4 Psalm 23
A SONG FOR DARK DAYS

THE BIG IDEA

God is with us even on dark days.

SUMMARY

Psalm 23 celebrates the provision and security which we have from God. God is our Shepherd (v 1-4) and our host (v 5-6). This is our comfort and confidence. The goodness of knowing God and the promise of dwelling with him forever outweigh the darkness of present circumstances—even the "valley of the shadow of death" or "darkest valley". We can know that God is present with us on dark days.

The psalm personalises the experience of God's people (see table on next page. What

God has done for his people, he has done for *me*. Jesus is *my* shepherd and *my* host.

God is described as the Shepherd of Israel (Genesis 49 v 24)	Now David talks of God as "my shepherd" (v 1)
When Jeremiah speaks of God leading his people through the wilderness, he talks about it as "the shadow of death" (Jeremiah 2 v 6, NKJV).	Now David talks of God leading him through the valley of the shadow of death or "darkest valley" (v 4).
God's rod parted the Red Sea and brought water from the rock (Exodus 14 v 16 and 17 v 5-6).	Now David says that God comforts him with his rod (v 4).
Psalm 78 implies that the LORD spread a table for them in the desert when the rock was struck with God's rod (Psalm 78 v 18-20).	Now David says that God has prepared a table for him (v 5).

GUIDANCE FOR QUESTIONS

1. Think about a dark time in your life. How did you find comfort in your situation? You might like to go first, to "break the ice" for others.

2. What does God do for David? He provides for David's needs (v 1-2); he restores David's soul (v 3); he guides the way in which David lives, enabling him to live righteously (v 3); he comforts David in dark and frightening situations (v 4).

3. David uses the picture of a shepherd caring for his sheep to describe God. Rewrite verses 1-4 using an image from our day. Some may find this task difficult, while others will really enjoy it. Put people into pairs or small groups and give ideas if necessary.

4. What do you think David meant by "the valley of the shadow of death" or "darkest valley"? What does this picture suggest to you? Generally this is used metaphorically of darkness (as dark as death, or the deepest darkness), but it sometimes means death itself (Job 38 v 17). So the valley of the shadow of death is an image for a dark and difficult situation—maybe one in which death is a real possibility.

5. APPLY: How can we experience the blessings of v 1-3 when we are going through the darkness of v 4? God doesn't promise to take us out of the difficult situation, but the psalm tells us that knowing that God is present with us in dark times will bring us through them. Note that it is God himself who is our blessing—even when circumstances are not happy. And he will guide us safely home to heaven. God's new creation will be a place of perfect peace, provision and restoration.

EXPLORE MORE

What did the staff of God do for his people (Exodus 14 v 13-31; 17 v 1-7)? It parted the Red Sea, delivering the Israelites from the Egyptian army, and provided water from the rock. It was the same staff that brought judgment on the Nile when God turned it into blood (Exodus 7 v 14-21). In Exodus 17 God is angry with the people because of their grumbling. But the rod of judgment falls on the rock instead of the people.

How does this verse (1 Corinthians 10 v 4) help us see the bigger picture of what is being shown here?

What did it mean for David to find comfort in God's rod and staff?

What does it mean for us? Paul says Jesus was that rock (1 Corinthians 10 v 4). God's judgment falls on Jesus instead of us. As a result, living water flows from Jesus (see John 7 v 37-39). David found comfort in remembering God's salvation and provision for God's people in the past. We, too, find comfort in remembering the work of Jesus and the blessings it brings.

EXPLORE MORE

(In Ezekiel 34 v 1-24) Who are the shepherds of Israel?
What is the problem with them?
What does God promise to do in response?
Through whom will God fulfil this promise (compare v 11 with v 23)? The shepherds of Israel are its leaders. But they have not cared for the people. Instead, they have exploited them. So God promises to remove the false shepherds. Instead, God will gather the people and care for them. In v 11 God says that he himself will do this. In v 23 he says he will do this through a new David, the Shepherd-King. This apparent discrepancy is resolved in Jesus, the Good Shepherd, who is both the Son of God and the Son of David (Romans 1 v 3-4).

6. What blessings does Jesus, the good Shepherd, provide for his people? He promises to care for his flock, protect them and give them life. When Jesus says he is the good Shepherd, he is claiming to be the Shepherd-King promised in Ezekiel 34. The blessings he brings are those described in Ezekiel 34 v 11-16.

- **How does he provide them?** By laying down his life for his people (v 11, 15).
- **How do we receive them?** Verse 16—by responding to his voice.

- **How do we hear the voice of the good Shepherd?** In the gospel message. So responding to the voice of the good Shepherd = faith in the gospel.

7. APPLY: How can we find comfort in Jesus, the good Shepherd, when we have dark days? This is an opportunity for people to share how the truth that Jesus is our good Shepherd has made an actual difference to real-life frightening or distressing situations. If no one is able to share in this way, discuss how comforting this image of Jesus can be. Why not contrast other religious or commonly-held views of God and compare how much, or how little comfort they give?

8. In verses 5-6 the picture changes from God as our shepherd to God as our host. Rewrite verses 5-6 with an image from our day. Put people into pairs or small groups and give ideas if necessary.

9. What does it mean for goodness and love to follow us? What does it mean for goodness and mercy to follow us into the valley of darkness? Even in the valley of darkness we can be confident that God is good and loving towards us. This may not seem apparent to us at the time—but we need to cling on to this fact because God's promise is more sure and real than the trouble we are experiencing. The idea that God's goodness and mercy will follow us suggests that we cannot escape God's blessing, even if we try. (The following questions on Romans 8 elaborate on this theme.)

10. How do these verses expand our understanding of Psalm 23 v 5-6?

- **What does Paul say about God's goodness?** God works for our good in every situation.

- **What is "the good" that God works for us?** We are conformed to the likeness of his Son.
- **What are our enemies, and how does God bless us in the face of these enemies?** Our enemies are anything or anyone who might condemn us: Satan, our sin, other people. But God blesses us with justification—he makes us right in his sight (even though we are sinners) through Jesus. Verses 35 and 38-39 list those things which threaten us, but none of them can separate us from God's love.
- **How does Paul express David's conviction that we "will dwell in the house of the LORD for ever"?** Paul is confident nothing can separate us from God's love. We can know God's love in this life whatever our circumstances. And we can be confident that we will enjoy his presence for ever in the new creation.

11. APPLY: Psalm 23 expresses calm confidence in the face of a dark situation. Where does David get this confidence from? How can we imitate him? Encourage people to focus on the truth about God that gives David confidence. Discuss how we can focus or refocus on these truths when we go through the dark times. If you looked at the Explore More on the staff of God, then you can add that David looks back to God's salvation in the past. For us, this is focused on the cross, when God's judgment fell on Christ our Rock.

12. APPLY: Think of some practical ways in which we can live our lives "in the house of the LORD". The house of the LORD is probably a reference to the temple. The temple was the focus of God's presence among his people. Dwelling in the house of the LORD is an image of living in God's company. The church is also described as God's temple (1 Peter 2 v 4-5). The temple was the place where the people met to praise God.

---

5 Psalm 27

A SONG FOR WHEN WE ARE AFRAID

THE BIG IDEA

We do not need to be afraid because God protects his people and provides for them.

SUMMARY

We're not sure of the context of this psalm, but it seems that David was under some sort of attack, probably a military one (v 2-3). He was also being falsely accused (v 12). The fact that the context is not specific may be significant. This is a psalm for God's people whenever they have any reason to fear.

In verses 1-6 of Psalm 27, David seems to speak to himself. As we have seen in these studies, we are to speak the truth about God to our hearts when we have reason to doubt or despair. We are to "preach" to ourselves. David reminds himself that God is his light, his salvation and his stronghold (v 1, 5-6). This gives him confidence in the face of threats (v 3). He also reminds himself that knowing God is the best thing and no one can take this from him (v 4).

In verses 7-12, David speaks to God in prayer. Having affirmed that God protects him, he now prays for God to protect him. He also prays that God will teach him and guide him (v 11). This is because fear often leads to sinful behaviour.

In verses 13-14, David summarises the psalm with some instructions to his readers.

We do not need to fear loss or harm when we delight in the goodness of God, because a relationship with God is better than anything else we might lose (v 13). When we have reason to fear, we should turn to God for help in prayer (v 14).

OPTIONAL EXTRA

Use the internet to create a "phobia quiz". Find some unusual phobias and see if people can guess what they are (perhaps with multiple choice answers). Use the quiz to introduce Q1.

GUIDANCE FOR QUESTIONS

1. What are you afraid of? Allow people to give both frivolous answers ("I'm afraid of spiders") and serious answers ("I fear rejection").

2. What can we know about David's situation from the psalm? We are not told the context in which this psalm was written. But the psalm itself suggests David was attacked by evil men (v 2), probably in the form of a military conflict (v 3). He was being falsely accused and threatened with violence (v 12).

3. Look at v 1-6. Who is David speaking to, do you think? Probably to himself.

4. Look at verses 1-3. What does David feel in this situation? Confident, despite being under attack. He refuses to be afraid.

5. What is the reason for David's confidence? See verse 1.

6. Look at verses 4-6. What is the one big thing that David seeks? To dwell in God's house forever. He wants to be able to know God and see His glory.

7. APPLY: We are often afraid because we are worried about what we might lose. How does knowing God help us overcome this fear? We will not be so worried about what we might lose if we have the best thing ie: a relationship with God (and no one can take it away from us—see Romans 8 v 35-39). We can gaze on the beauty of the LORD all the days of our life (v 4)—and the life to come.

8. APPLY: We are often afraid because of what might happen to us. How does knowing God help us overcome this fear? God promises to protect us. Even if he does not deliver us from our immediate problems, he will keep us safe in his presence now and in eternity (v 5).

9. APPLY: David begins this psalm by talking to himself. What should we tell ourselves when we are afraid? This is an opportunity to summarise what we have learned so far.

10. Look at verses 7-12. Who is David talking to in these verses? God.

11. What does David say about God in verses 7-12? God is personal and knowable—David understands the possibility of having a conversation with God (v 7) and seeking God's face (v 8); God is David's Helper and Saviour (v 9); God can teach David (v 11); God is good (v 13).

12. What does David ask God in verses 7-12? David asks God to:
- hear, be merciful and answer him (v 7)
- not reject him (v 9)
- teach him (v 11)
- not give him over to his enemies (v 12)

13. APPLY: How should we pray when we feel afraid? This is an opportunity to summarise and apply what you have learned from verses 7-12.

14. One of the things we often fear is rejection. We worry about what other people think of us. We "need" their approval. Look at verses 8-10. What answer does David give for this kind of fear?

- **Where does David say we should look? How does this help us overcome our fear of other people?**

David reminds us that God's approval is more important than the approval of other people. We need to fear God more than we fear other people. And God has promised to receive us in Christ's name. He will not turn away from us in anger, as people often do (v 9), because Christ has taken God's anger against us on himself, on the cross.

15. How does fear affect our behaviour? Why does David pray as he does in verse 11? Fear often leads to sin. We succumb to peer pressure, or tell lies to cover up, or exaggerate to impress. See if you can think of other examples of fear leading to sin. David asks God to teach him and lead him so that he will not sin in the face of fear.

16. Look at verses 13-14. What should we do when we are afraid? This is an opportunity to summarise what we have learned throughout the psalm. Verses 13-14 seem to be a summary of the psalm. (1) In verse 13 we are reminded that we do not need to be afraid of loss or harm when we delight in the goodness of God, because a relationship with God is better than anything else we might lose and no one can take it from us. (2) In verse 14 we are reminded that we should turn to God for help. To wait on God = to look to God for help.

17. APPLY: How can we help one another overcome our fear?
Make the link with the answer to question 16. We help one another by (1) reminding one another of God's goodness and (2) praying with one another for God's help. Discuss the practicalities of how you can do these things.

Note: The "Optional Extra" at the end of Session Six needs preparing beforehand, and you might like to mention it at the end of this study.

6 Psalm 32

A SONG FOR SECRET GUILT

THE BIG IDEA

Hiding or denying our sin leads to psychological and even physical sickness. Confessing our sin leads to forgiveness and blessing.

SUMMARY

Psalm 32 describes what happens when we deny or hide sin. It leads to psychological and even physical sickness. Our modern culture says the answer is to downplay or ignore sin, but this does not bring health. Freedom and joy are found in acknowledging sin before God and receiving his forgiveness.

Verses 1-2 describe the opposite, healthy situation. God blesses sinners who acknowledge their sin before him. The problems come for people who pretend they are not sinners. David suffers when he does not acknowledge his sin (= denies sin) and covers up his iniquity (= hides sin) (verses 3-5). He finds forgiveness only when he confesses his sin to God (verse 5). So his advice is not to be a stubborn mule (= to refuse to come to God for forgiveness) (verses 8-10).

Instead, we should seek God in prayer and repentance (verses 5-7).

GUIDANCE FOR QUESTIONS

1. What attitude do people in general have towards sin? The theme of this psalm is not easy to talk about specifically in a group, because the theme is unconfessed or secret sin. This talkabout question allows people to get talking without being personal or specific.

- **How does our society talk about sin?**

2. What do people say we should do if we feel guilty? Our society often sees a sense of guilt as a bad thing. It treats guilt as something to be ignored or avoided. It does this by passing the blame or denying that sin is serious. "Don't worry about it," people commonly say when others express a sense of guilt.

3. Look at verses 1-2. How does David define blessing? As forgiveness from God for our sins.

4. Who does God bless? Sinners, by forgiving their sins. This may seem an obvious statement, but it prepares the way for the central theme of the psalm, which is the problems created by hiding or denying our sin. God does not bless "righteous" people; He blesses sinners (see Mark 2 v 17). We find blessing not by hiding our sin, but by confessing our sin. The one "in whose spirit is no deceit" (v 2) is not an honest person *per se*, but a person who is honest about their sin.

5. Look at verses 3-5. What was David silent about? See verse 5. Relief comes when David acknowledges his sin and does not cover up his iniquity. So, presumably, he had previously not acknowledged sin and had hidden his iniquity.

6. What happens when we deny or hide our sin? See v 3-4. Unconfessed sin leads to psychological and even physical sickness.

Verse 4 suggests that this sickness came from God ("your hand was heavy on me"). Psalm 38 also suggests sickness can be the result of God's discipline.

7. What happens when we confess our sin to the Lord? See v 5. God forgives our sin. Look back at verses 1-2; God blesses us.

EXPLORE MORE

(In Psalm 38) What effect does sin have on David? He is pierced—there is no health or soundness in his body, he is burdened with guilt, he is brought low, he is crushed, he groans in anguish, he is deserted by his friends and people gloat over him.
How does David respond to the situation he is in (see verses 18 and 21-22)? He sees this sickness as him being afflicted by God and responds by confessing his sin and asking God to help him.
How does God discipline us today? On God's discipline, see Hebrews 12 v 4-11. Sickness is sometimes the result of God's discipline (see 1 Corinthians 11 v 27-32 and James 5 v 14-16).
Is sickness always a result of God's discipline? There is not necessarily a direct link between particular sins and sickness (see John 9 v 1-3). However, God uses everything in our life—including sickness—to make us more like Jesus (Romans 8 v 28-29).

8. APPLY: In what ways do we try to deny or hide our sin? We pass the blame: we blame other people, our circumstances, our genes or our up-bringing. We downplay our sin: we make out it is not too serious or that it is was inevitable.

9. APPLY: What consequences have you seen in individuals when they have tried to deny or hide their sin? What consequences do we see in society when people try to ignore the reality of sin? This is an opportunity to learn from the real-life experiences of others. Do warn the group not to breach the confidentiality of others.

10. Look at verses 6-7. What is David's remedy for the problem of secret sin? To seek God in prayer (v 6). Specifically, we are to confess our sin to him and find forgiveness from him (v 5). We take refuge in God (v 7).

11. David says that God will protect us if we confess our sin. How does confession lead to protection? From what are we protected? Secret sin, we have seen, leads to psychological and even physical sickness. Confession and forgiveness from God set us free from this. Secret sin also makes us afraid of exposure and shame. But the ultimate threat facing us is God's judgment. If we deny or hide our sin, then we can have no assurance. But if we confess our sin, then God promises to protect us from his own judgment.

EXPLORE MORE

What Bible story involves "mighty waters" that "rise" (v 6)? The flood in Genesis 6 – 9.
What were the rising waters a sign or consequence of in the story? The rising waters were a sign and consequence of God's judgment (Genesis 6 v 5-7).
How do we escape the rising waters? Through faith in Jesus (1 Peter 3 v 20-21). Jesus bore God's judgment in our place.

12. Look at verses 8-11. What advice does David give to us? The context of the psalm as a whole suggests David wants us to learn from his experience. He wants us not to hide or deny our sin, but confess it and turn back to God. In v 8-11 he advises us to trust in God's unfailing love (v 10) and rejoice in him (v 11).

13. How can we be like a stubborn mule (v 9)? By refusing to turn to God in confession and repentance. We shrink from God because we do not trust his love and forgiveness. We do not come near to him because we are afraid of him or because we do not delight in him. But the truth is that God's unfailing love surrounds those who turn to him in faith.

14. APPLY: Is it good to feel guilty? Should we encourage people to feel guilty? This psalm shows that unaddressed guilt can lead to psychological and physical sickness. But the answer is not to pretend we are not guilty (by passing the blaming or not taking sin seriously). The answer is to acknowledge our guilt and find forgiveness in Christ.

Acknowledging guilt ⊖ repentance ⊖ freedom and forgiveness.

Suppressing guilt ⊖ no repentance ⊖ no freedom and no forgiveness.

We may need to confront people with their guilt so they can find freedom and forgiveness through repentance.

15. APPLY: How do we hide sin in the church? What effect does this have on the Christian community? We often pretend that we are all doing well in our Christian lives. People do not feel able to talk about their struggles. We become communities of law rather than communities of grace. The world thinks we are self-righteous and Christians think they must struggle alone.

- **What can our church or home group do to be more honest and grace-centred?**

16. APPLY: What value is there in confessing our sin to another person? David confesses his sin to the Lord. But he also tells us about the experience in this psalm. Confessing to other people is not necessary to receive forgiveness from God. But many people find it helpful. It marks a clear break with secret sin. And the person to whom we confess can remind us of God's grace and promises.

OPTIONAL EXTRA

God gives "songs of deliverance" to those who find forgiveness in him (v 7). David's final exhortation is to "sing" (v 11). Many great hymns and songs have been written that celebrate God's forgiveness. At the end of the previous session, or a few days before you meet, ask people to choose a favourite song or poem on the theme of forgiveness. Whether you sing them might depend on the musical abilities of your group! You could, however, use them as a basis of prayer and praise.

At The Good Book Company, we are dedicated to helping Christians and local churches grow. We believe that God's growth process always starts with hearing clearly what he has said to us through his timeless word—the Bible.

Ever since we opened our doors in 1991, we have been striving to produce resources that honour God in the way the Bible is used. We have grown to become an international provider of user-friendly resources to the Christian community, with believers of all backgrounds and denominations using our Bible studies, books, evangelistic resources, DVD-based courses and training events.

We want to equip ordinary Christians to live for Christ day by day, and churches to grow in their knowledge of God, their love for one another, and the effectiveness of their outreach.

Call us for a discussion of your needs or visit one of our local websites for more information on the resources and services we provide.

Your friends at The Good Book Company

UK & EUROPE		thegoodbook.co.uk		0333 123 0880
NORTH AMERICA		thegoodbook.com		866 244 2165
AUSTRALIA		thegoodbook.com.au		(02) 6100 4211
NEW ZEALAND		thegoodbook.co.nz		(+64) 3 343 2463

WWW.CHRISTIANITYEXPLORED.ORG
Our partner site is a great place for those exploring the Christian faith, with a clear explanation of the good news, powerful testimonies and answers to difficult questions.